Discovery Biographies

Aviators
Amelia Earhart
Charles Lindbergh

**Conservationists
and Naturalists**
Rachel Carson

Educators
Mary McLeod Bethune
Booker T. Washington

Entertainers
Annie Oakley
The Ringling Brothers

Explorers
Juan Ponce de León
Marco Polo

First Ladies
Abigail Adams
Mary Todd Lincoln
Dolly Madison
Martha Washington

Government Leaders
Henry Clay

Military Heroes
David G. Farragut
Robert E. Lee
Paul Revere

Nurses and Doctors
Clara Barton
Elizabeth Blackwell
Florence Nightingale

**Pioneers and
Frontiersmen**
Jim Beckwourth
Daniel Boone
Jim Bridger
Davy Crockett
John Smith

Poets
Francis Scott Key

Presidents
Andrew Jackson
Abraham Lincoln
Harry S. Truman

**Engineers
and Inventors**
George W. Goethals
Samuel F. B. Morse
Eli Whitney

Social Reformers
Dorothea Dix
Frederick Douglass
Helen Keller

CHELSEA HOUSE PUBLISHERS

A Discovery Biography

Florence Nightingale

—◆—

War Nurse

by Anne Colver

illustrated by Gerald McCann

CHELSEA JUNIORS

A division of Chelsea House Publishers

New York • Philadelphia

The Discovery Biographies have been prepared under the
educational supervision of Mary C. Austin, Ed.D.,
reading specialist and professor of education, Case
Western Reserve University.

Cover illustration: Marjorie Zaum

First Chelsea House edition 1992

3   5   7   9   8   6   4   2

ISBN   0-7910-1466-5

Contents

Florence Nightingale:
War Nurse

Chapter *1*

Playing Nurse

One summer afternoon a little girl sat beside a row of dolls. She was pretending the dolls were sick in a hospital. She was their nurse. "Sh-sh," she whispered. "Jennie-Marie is very sick. We must be quiet. And poor Florabel may have to have an *operation!*"

The little girl was very pretty. She had red-brown curls and big gray eyes. Her name was Florence Nightingale.

She lived in a big stone house called Lea Hurst. It was in the south of England. This was the year 1827. Florence was seven years old.

Florence was very gentle with the poor, sick dolls. Some of them were hers. Some belonged to her sister Parthe. Florence tucked the covers over them. "I will take care of you and make you well," she promised.

Suddenly a voice interrupted Florence. Nanny was speaking. Nanny took care of Florence and Parthe when their mother was busy with parties and friends. "Come now, Miss Flo," Nanny said. "You have played hospital long enough. Your mother is having ladies for tea. She wants you to put on your best dress and meet them."

"I won't leave my dolls. They are sick!" Florence stamped her foot. "I *won't* meet Mamma's guests!"

Florence was not being naughty. She was a shy child. It frightened her to meet strange people. They patted her on the head. They asked how old she was. Often she was too frightened to answer.

Florence ran to the window. Her gray eyes were dark and stormy. She looked across the green lawns and the gardens to the stables. She knew her white pony, Duchess, was waiting in the stable. "If I can't play hospital, please let me ride Duchess," Florence begged.

Nanny shook her head. "You must obey your mamma, Miss Flo," she said.

"Why can't you be a little lady, like your sister Parthe?"

Parthe stood waiting in her white dress. Her hair was brushed smoothly. "Come along, Flo," Parthe said. "Don't be so babyish."

Florence did not argue any more. She put on her best dress. She followed Parthe downstairs. Her mother's guests were beautiful. Their silk skirts rustled. Parthe curtsied and smiled politely. Florence curtsied too. But she was not happy. Her heart pounded with shyness and misery.

"If I could only be upstairs with the sick dolls that need me," Florence thought.

Chapter *2*

Animal Patients

When Florence was older she nursed sick animals instead of dolls.

The Nightingale family had many pets. The two ponies, Duchess and Lady, belonged to Florence and Parthe. Flo also had a shaggy dog named Max. Parthe's white cat, Snowball, had little kittens every summer. And there were rabbits and turtles and cages of pet birds.

Florence and her sister loved to take care of the pets. Sometimes Flo pretended the kittens and puppies were sick. She bandaged their paws and gave them sugar and water for medicine.

One day Florence was in the yard feeding some of her pets. The old gardener, Pat, came by. He was carrying his collie dog. The dog's leg was bleeding. Pat was very upset. "A fox just bit Rags, Miss Flo," he said. "His poor leg is all torn. You are always playing nurse. Can you help Rags, please?"

Florence looked at the dog's leg. "I think I can help him," she said quietly. "Bring me hot water and clean cloths." She bandaged the dog's leg carefully. "Leave Rags here," she said to Pat. "I will take care of him."

The old man nodded. He trusted Florence.

The dog was well in a few days. Pat was very happy. He told his friends what Miss Flo had done. Other people around Lea Hurst began to bring their sick animals to Florence. They brought sick lambs and chickens. There was a stray kitten. One little girl even brought a lame donkey. "Please help him, Miss Flo," she begged. "When he *hee-haws,* he sounds so sad."

"I will try to help," Florence said.

Florence's father and mother smiled. "It is nice that Flo is so kindhearted," they said. Mr. Nightingale let Florence use a corner of the big greenhouse for her animal hospital. Soon the corner was filled with patients.

"How do you know how to cure these animals?" Florence's father asked.

"I don't," Florence answered honestly. "I just feed them and keep them comfortable. And I love them. And most of them get well."

Mr. and Mrs. Nightingale smiled again. "Flo has always liked to play nurse," they agreed. They did not know that Florence dreamed of being a real nurse someday.

Chapter *3*

"Let Me Help"

Florence was always sad when summer was over. Then the Nightingales left Lea Hurst. The rest of the year they lived near the big city of London.

One time the trunks were all packed. The carriages were waiting to take the family to London. Suddenly Florence could not be found. "Flo," her father called. "Where are you, Flo?"

19

Finally he found Florence in the garden. She was kissing a rosebush. "You have already hugged each horse in the stables," her father told Florence patiently. "You have patted every cow and sheep and pig. Now why are you kissing every bush?"

"Because I must tell them good-by too," Florence answered solemnly. "I promise each one of them I will come back next summer. Then they won't miss me so much."

Florence was always homesick for Lea Hurst. She missed the wide, free countryside. She was unhappy in the crowded city. Her parents had more fashionable parties there. That meant more guests to dress up for.

The Nightingales traveled so much that Flo and Parthe could not go to regular school. They had lessons from private teachers. Their father was their most important teacher. He made them work hard. He was very strict. Sometimes Parthe would throw down her book and rush to her mother. "Papa makes us work too long," she would wail.

However, Florence never complained. "I will work until I *finish*," she said.

Florence found many things to study besides her lessons. She was always watching people. She worried when she thought other people were unhappy. "Miss Flo is too sensitive," Nanny said. "She must get over these foolish ideas."

But Flo went on worrying. She worried because her family was rich and others were poor. She worried most about poor people who were sick. They had no one to take care of them.

One day in London, Florence was riding in the carriage with her father and mother. They passed a beggar woman with a little boy. The boy's thin hands were stretched out to her. His bare feet were blue with cold.

Florence leaned out of the carriage. "Let me help. Please let me help the little boy," she begged. "He's sick—"

The Nightingale's carriage moved on.

That night Florence could not go to sleep. She kept thinking of the thin little boy.

She wished she could take him home to Lea Hurst. "I would take care of him and make him well," she sobbed. "I want to help all the poor sick children in the world."

Mr. Nightingale tried to comfort Florence. "Don't cry, Flo," he said gently. "Some people must always be poor. You are too little to worry about the world. It will never be any better."

Florence jumped up to face her tall father. Her small feet were planted wide apart. "Then I will change it," Florence told him. *I will make the world better.*

Chapter *4*

Secret Friends

The summer Florence was fourteen her family traveled to the country as usual. Florence was excited as they drove through the village near Lea Hurst. She leaned out of the carriage, waving happily. "Hello, Mr. Jenkins," she called to the blacksmith.

"Welcome, Miss Flo," he answered with a broad smile.

The carriage passed many farm cottages. Florence greeted the farmers and their wives. She remembered all the children's names. When she spoke to them, they waved back. Even the rough-looking shepherds touched their caps to "Miss Flo."

"Oh, look — there's Mr. Henley," Florence pointed to a lame old man. "I was afraid he wouldn't live through the winter. He has dreadful rheumatism."

The old man raised his cane to her in greeting.

Mr. and Mrs. Nightingale were surprised. "How do all these people know Flo?" Mrs. Nightingale asked.

There was a good reason why they knew Florence.

Mrs. Nightingale often sent food to the village people. Florence took it for her. She would fill her pony cart with baskets of fresh eggs and cream and fruit. Florence's mother told her to leave the baskets for any poor people who were sick. But Florence did not just *leave* the baskets. She stopped to visit each sick person. She helped take care of them. She talked to the old people and rocked the new babies.

Her village friends loved Florence. "Miss Flo can cure sick people better than medicine," they said. But Florence never told her family. She was afraid they might scold her for having more "foolish ideas." She kept her new friends secret.

That summer Florence went on taking baskets of food to the cottages. She visited all the sick people.

One night something happened that gave Florence's secret away. There was a knock at the Nightingale's front door. Mr. Nightingale went to answer. A farmer stood outside.

"Please, sir," the farmer said. "My boy Georgie had a bad accident. His knee is hurt and swollen. He's begging for Miss Florence. We all know how Miss Flo can help sick people. Can she come help Georgie, please?"

Mr. Nightingale was astonished. He could not imagine his daughter nursing a farmer's child. Before he could answer, Florence hurried past him. "I must go, Georgie needs my help," Florence said.

Mr. Nightingale stood back. He was still astonished. But he saw a determined look in Florence's gray eyes. He knew he could not stop her.

Florence stayed with the sick boy that night. Day after day she visited him. She put hot bandages on his knee. She comforted him when the pain was bad. Finally his knee was better.

Florence was happy. She told her father and mother that Georgie was almost well.

Florence did not forget Georgie, or the other sick people she helped. At last she said, "I want to work in a hospital and make more people well."

Her parents were upset. "You cannot do that," they told Florence. "No *nice* young ladies work in hospitals!"

Florence's mother and father were right. In those days hospitals were crowded, dirty places. There were no schools to train nurses. The only "nurses" were women who could not find any other work.

"You will never need to work," Florence's mother and father told her. "You will have plenty of money. You will have every comfort at home."

They did not understand that Florence *wanted* to work.

Chapter 5

A Happy Birthday

Florence had grown into a beautiful young lady. She was slim and graceful. Her red-brown hair curled around her delicate face. Florence and Parthe were invited to many parties.

They were even invited to the Royal Palace by England's new Queen Victoria. The Queen was very young herself. She was only one year older than Florence. Florence curtsied to the young queen.

In years to come both girls would play important parts in history. They would often meet again.

Many people noticed the beautiful and popular Miss Flo. Mr. and Mrs. Nightingale were pleased. "Thank goodness, Flo is getting over being shy," Mrs. Nightingale said. "Young gentlemen are beginning to admire her. She will soon forget about wanting to be a nurse."

Mrs. Nightingale was right. Many young men admired Florence. One young man, Richard Milnes, fell deeply in love with her. He begged Florence to marry him. Florence could not decide. She was in love with Richard. She wanted to marry him and be happy. But she could not give up her dream of being a nurse.

Richard waited a long time. He loved Florence very much. Finally he said, "You must choose, Flo. Choose your work — or me."

Florence shook her head. There were tears in her eyes. "I was not born to *choose*," she said. "I was born to do a special work. *I must work.* I must give up everything else—even you, Richard."

Florence's family was shocked. They could not believe she would give up a fine young man for more of her "foolish ideas." They were disappointed in Florence.

Florence was very unhappy because her parents would not let her be a nurse. She thought about it so much that she became ill. Her parents sent her away to get well. But she was still miserable.

The next spring Florence met Dr. Elizabeth Blackwell, who was visiting from America. Dr. Blackwell was the first American woman to study medicine. She was a real doctor.

Now Florence was more determined than ever. "Elizabeth Blackwell can be a doctor. Why can't I be a nurse?" she demanded. Then she learned about a hospital in Germany where girls could study nursing.

"Please let me go," Florence begged her father and mother. At last they agreed.

One May morning, just before her birthday, Florence started for Germany. It was the happiest birthday she had ever had.

Chapter *6*

Nursing School

A doctor and his wife ran the hospital in Germany. They greeted Florence kindly. They gave her a blue cotton uniform and a white apron. They showed her an iron cot where she would sleep. It was very different from Florence's comfortable bed at home.

"We need another nurse in the children's ward tonight," the doctor said. "Can you help?"

Florence was very tired, but she nodded quickly. "Of course, I will help."

The hospital had men and women patients. There was also a building for orphans and sick children. The work was hard. *"We get up at five o'clock in the morning,"* Florence wrote home. *"We have only ten minutes for each meal. The food is very plain. We only have bread and tea and vegetables."* But Florence was happy because she loved the work.

The doctors at the hospital saw that Florence was anxious to learn. They taught her to give medicines and treatments. They showed her how to help at operations. The sick children loved Florence especially. Each child was allowed to have a birthday party.

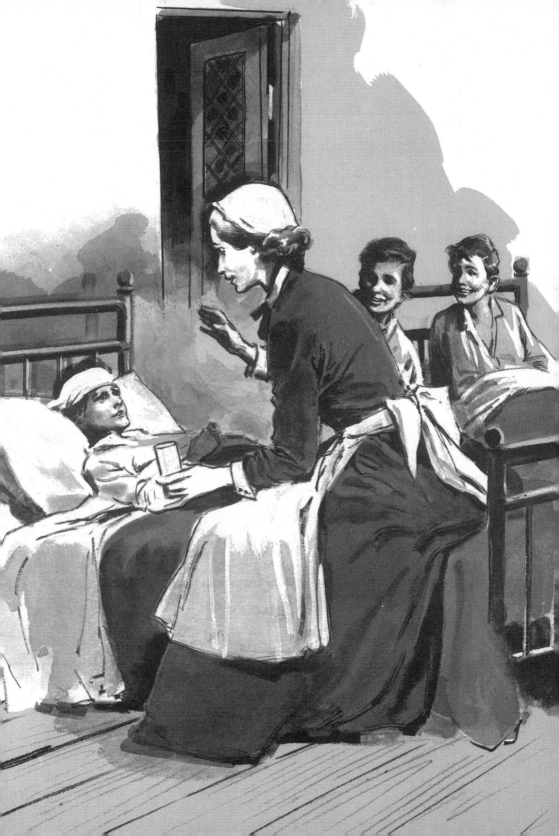

Florence was always invited to their parties. They looked forward to having her there. She was gay and full of fun.

When Florence left the hospital, the head doctor said, *"We have never had a nurse as intelligent and skillful as Miss Nightingale."*

Years later Florence wrote: *"I was never shy after I worked at the hospital in Germany. We learned to think of our work, not ourselves."*

When Florence came back to London she was offered a good job. She was head of a hospital for women. She nursed her patients carefully. She knew that loving care was as important as medicine. One patient wrote to Miss Nightingale: *"You were our sunshine."*

The doctors in London soon heard about Florence's work. "We should have nurses like Miss Nightingale in all our hospitals," they said. "Our patients would get well faster." The doctors asked Florence to teach other girls to be nurses. This was Florence's great dream. But before she could start a nurses' school, a war broke out.

The war changed everything.

Chapter 7

Off to War

War had started because Russia was trying to take land away from the country of Turkey. England and France did not think Russia was right. They tried to push Russia back.

They were fighting in a place called Crimea. It is across the Black Sea from Turkey.

English soldiers, in bright new uniforms, marched through the streets of London.

Florence was in the crowd that cheered them. They sailed bravely off to war.

But a few weeks later there were terrible stories in the newspapers. A newspaper man named Russell had been to the battlefields in Turkey. He wrote home: *"More than a thousand men were killed or wounded in the first battles. A thousand more are sick and dying with fever. The Army doctors are working hard. But there is no one to take care of the sick men."*

People in England were shocked by the stories. They thought of their husbands and sons and brothers lying on the battlefields. "We must help our soldiers," they said. "The War Department must send someone to take care of them."

The head of the War Department was Sir Sidney Herbert. He was an old friend of Florence's. He knew what a wonderful nurse Florence was. He wrote to Florence, *"You are the one person who can help our soldiers."*

When Florence got the letter she hurried to see Sidney Herbert. "I will go," she told him.

Plans were made. Florence was to take forty nurses to the Crimea with her. "How soon can you leave?" Sir Sidney asked.

"In one week," Florence answered quickly.

It was a busy week. Florence finished her work at the London hospital. She bought supplies and uniforms for the nurses.

Florence's father and mother and her sister Parthe came to London. They helped Florence get ready to leave. They forgot they had tried to keep Florence from being a nurse. Now there were stories in the newspapers about Florence every day. Her family was proud of her.

The most important thing Florence had to do was choose nurses to go with her. Many women wanted to go. Some she chose were rough women who had nursed in London hospitals. Some were gentle Catholic Sisters, who had been trained to nurse. Florence did not care where they came from. She wanted the ones who would nurse best. She knew they must be able to face many hardships.

The newspapers wrote about the *"brave Miss Nightingale and her nurses going to war."* One newspaper said there should be a parade to see the nurses off. Florence shook her head. *"I am not afraid to go to war,"* she told Sir Sidney. *"But I am NOT brave enough to stand a fuss. Please let us leave quietly."*

Sidney Herbert understood. "You and your nurses will leave London as quietly as forty mice," he promised.

Sir Sidney kept his promise. The night of October 21, 1854, was dark. No one noticed when forty women slipped on board a ship at the docks. They were dressed in brown cloaks. The smallest figure was in the front of the line. It was Florence.

The next day the London papers told
how Miss Nightingale and her nurses
had left. They said: *"The prayers of all
England go with them."*

Chapter 8

A Hospital for Soldiers

The nurses had a long, hard trip to Crimea. They traveled more than a month, partly by ship and partly by land. The weather was cold and stormy. Most of the women were seasick.

Finally, on a November afternoon, they landed at Constantinople. This city was across the Black Sea from Crimea where the war was being fought.

The nurses stood on the deck of the ship. They shivered in the icy wind. Florence stood with them.

At home, Florence had always hated cold weather. Her sister Parthe used to tease her and say, "Flo shivers and shakes until her bones rattle when a cool breeze blows!" Yet Florence did not shiver now. Her face was pale. But she stood straight.

The ship's captain spoke to Florence. He pointed to a huge, shabby wooden building on a hill. "There's the hospital, ma'am," he said. "It used to be an old barracks house. It was deserted for years. Then our Army people took it for their sick soldiers. I've heard they found nothing inside except dirt — and rats."

Florence only nodded. But a new shiver went through the nurses when they heard the word *rats*.

A few minutes later the women were on shore. There was no one to meet them. They would have to carry their luggage up the steep hill. A few of the nurses grumbled. But just then they saw wounded soldiers being taken off another ship. The men were ragged and dirty and cold. Some had bloody bandages on their arms or legs. Many of them could hardly walk. Some were too sick to move. They lay on the icy ground.

When they saw the poor soldiers, the nurses forgot how tired and sick they felt themselves. "Where have these men come from?" Florence asked a sailor.

"From a terrible battle, ma'am," he answered. "It was the bloodiest battle yet. There were hundreds killed and hurt. Plenty more wounded will be coming in soon, ma'am."

"We must get them to the hospital," Florence said. She went to help a soldier with a bandage over his eyes.

The other nurses hurried to help too. One who had grumbled loudest took off her cloak. She put it around a soldier who wore only a thin shirt. He was blue with cold. Slowly the nurses helped the soldiers climb up the hill.

The nurses found things even worse in the old barracks building. It was not a real hospital. There were no beds or blankets. The wounded men had to lie on the bare floors.

There were no fires to keep them warm. They had nothing to eat but half-raw meat and vegetables. There was hardly any water to drink or wash with.

Florence hurried to the Army officer in charge of the hospital. "We are here to help take care of your men," she said. "Tell us what to do."

The officer frowned. He was angry at the London newspapers. Their stories had said his hospital did not take good care of the soldiers. He was even angrier at the War Department for sending *women* to help. "The Army has never needed women," he told Florence coldly. "We do not need them now."

Florence went back to tell her nurses. They were very bitter and disappointed.

They knew how badly the soldiers were suffering. They wanted to start taking care of them right away. Florence shook her head. "We must wait until the officers *know* they need us," she said.

The tired nurses had only dry bread and tea for supper. The forty women were crowded into two bare, dirty rooms to sleep. Their beds were hard wooden benches. Florence took a small closet for her own room. It was dark and stuffy. But she could work late at night there without disturbing the others.

Long after the nurses slept, Florence sat up writing letters. She wrote to Sidney Herbert in London. She told how the soldiers were suffering. *"The doctors are doing their best,"* she wrote.

"But there is no medicine or decent food. There are no beds. These brave men lie without care. We must find a way to help them . . ."

Chapter *9*

The Lady with the Lamp

The next morning Florence had an idea. "The Army officers don't want women *nurses*," she said. "But perhaps they would like women cooks!"

Florence and her nurses went into the hospital kitchen. They built a fire. They scrubbed dirty pots and pans. Then they made soups and jellies and hot, strong tea. They went through the hospital, feeding the sick soldiers. The sickest men took a bit of broth or tea.

They looked up gratefully when the nurses fed them. "Sometimes a few spoonfuls of hot food can save a man's life," Florence wrote to Sidney Herbert.

The doctors saw how much Florence and her nurses helped the men. "Let them stay and nurse if they can stand the work," the doctors said. "God bless them."

There were still some Army officers who did not want the women there. But the terrible battles went on. More and more wounded men were brought up the hill to the hospital. Even those officers saw that the nurses were needed now.

Florence worked hardest of all the nurses. At night she sat at her desk.

She wrote many letters for the soldiers to their families in England. Often she could send them good news. Sometimes she had to tell the family that a soldier had died. Florence sent many more letters to the War Department in London. *"The soldiers need warm blankets and clothes,"* she wrote. *"You MUST send more medicines and bandages. Many men are dying because we do not have these things . . ."*

Late at night Florence would leave her desk and walk through the long rows of sick men. She carried a lamp to light her way. Many soldiers could not sleep because of their pain. They watched for her lamp in the lonely dark. They called her *the Lady with the Lamp.*

Florence always seemed to know when a soldier was very sick. She would kneel beside him and try to help his pain. Sometimes a soldier was worried because he was going to have an operation. Florence would promise to stand by him in the operating room. One soldier said: "She was so brave herself, she gave us all courage."

Another soldier wrote: *"What comfort we felt to see her. We lay in the hospital by the hundreds . . . We kissed her shadow as she passed."*

One night Florence's lamp went out. There was no more oil in it. She went on walking. Suddenly she heard a sound of crying. She bent down. In the dim light, she saw a young boy's face.

Florence touched his cheek. "Are you in pain?" she asked.

"No, ma'am," the boy answered. He choked back a sob. "I'm only homesick, I guess. I'm ashamed—"

"Don't be ashamed," Florence said. "I miss my home too, and my family. How old are you?"

"Almost thirteen, ma'am. But please don't tell. I told them I was older to get in the army."

The boy's name was Bobby Robinson.

"You are still too young for fighting," Florence said. "When you get well, Bobby, you can stay here and work with me. You can run errands and carry food for the sick men."

"I'd like that, ma'am," the boy said. "I'll work as hard as anything for you."

When Bobby was well, he kept his promise. He followed Florence like a faithful shadow. He was too busy now to feel homesick. His proudest duty was to polish the lamp Florence carried through the hospital at night. He kept it filled with oil. It never went out again.

Chapter *10*

Fever

The letters Florence wrote to the War Department were printed in London. The English people read them. They said, "Miss Nightingale is right. Our soldiers *must* have better care."

Queen Victoria read Florence's letters too. The Queen herself wrote to Florence, *"Your goodness and devotion has been observed with highest admiration. Please tell the soldiers that their Queen thinks of them and prays for them every day."*

Soon after the Queen's letter Florence had more good news. The War Department sent the supplies she had asked for. When the food and medicines and blankets came, the soldiers began to get well faster.

At last the war ended. It was a victory for England and Turkey. The countries were ready to make peace with Russia. Florence could take a few days rest. She went to visit the battlefields in Crimea.

The sun was warm again. Flowers were blooming everywhere. Florence enjoyed the fresh spring air. She rode a pretty little horse over the battlefields. Whenever soldiers saw Florence ride past, they cheered her.

A few days later a terrible thing happened. Florence fainted. She was very sick. Four soldiers carried her to the hospital. Young Bobby walked beside her. He was crying for the first time since the night Florence had found him.

The doctors shook their heads. "Miss Nightingale has nursed hundreds of men with the fever," one said. "Now she may die of the fever herself."

When the soldiers heard how sick Miss Nightingale was, they prayed for her. The people in England prayed too.

At last Florence was better. Everyone was happy. Even strangers said to each other, "Have you heard the good news? Miss Nightingale is getting well." Queen Victoria wrote: *"We are truly thankful that Miss Nightingale is safe."*

When Florence could walk again, she was pale and weak. The doctors wanted Florence to go home to England and rest. But she would not go. Soon she was working again to help the soldiers get well.

Finally the time came for the soldiers and nurses to sail home. Florence said good-by to each one. Many of the nurses were in tears as they waved to Florence from the ship.

Mother Bermondsey, one of the Catholic sisters, wrote, *"We all worked long and hard during the war. We were always tired. Only Miss Nightingale never seemed tired. Her voice was always soft. Her smile was always beautiful. She kept us all working together."*

Chapter *11*

A Dream Come True

Finally Florence sailed for home. The people in England wanted to have a grand celebration to welcome her. Newspapers called her "The great heroine of the battlefields."

Florence did not want a celebration. "People are very kind," she smiled. "But I am too tired to feel like a great heroine. I only want to see my family again. And then rest."

So Florence came home quietly. She went to her beloved Lea Hurst to rest. Still the English people did not forget her. They wanted to thank her for all her help to the soldiers. They raised money to buy Miss Nightingale a gift. "We will let her choose the gift she wants most," they agreed.

Florence was very grateful. "I will use the money to start a school for nurses in London," she said. "That is the best gift I could ever have."

The Nightingale School was started the next year. Florence herself chose the girls for the first class. She planned every part of their training. She believed that nurses should study, as doctors did.

"When I learned to be a nurse in

Germany," she said, "I only learned to *work*. These girls must learn to *study* too."

The girls at the *Nightingale School* worked and studied very hard. They learned about the human body and sickness. They were the first really *trained* nurses in the world. Soon other nursing schools were started in England and all over the world. Florence's great dream had come true.

Florence was often ill after the war. She did not get completely well for many years. Still she never stopped working. The English government asked her for advice about health problems in India. "Give the people better food," Florence said. "Teach them to be clean, then they will be healthy."

Florence lived to be a very old lady. She had seen much suffering. She had had many troubles herself. But her last years were happy. When Florence was a little girl she had said, *"I will make the world better."* She had truly made it better. She had changed the world's ideas about nursing. She had trained other nurses to carry on her work.

Florence is still honored as the world's first great nurse. Her picture hangs on the wall in many hospitals. When young nurses go into training today, they look up at the beautiful face of Florence Nightingale.